Rus in Urbe

James Lawless

Rus in Urbe
is published by
DOGHOUSE
P.O. Box 312
Tralee G.P.O.
Co. Kerry
Ireland
TEL: +353 (0)66 7137547
www.doghousebooks.ie
email: doghouse312@eircom.net

© James Lawless 2012
ISBN 978-0-9572073-0-1

Edited for DOGHOUSE by Noel King

Cover illustration, *The Journey,* by Anne-Marie Glasheen
www.glasheen.co.uk

The poet and publisher thank Kildare
County Council for their financial
support towards this collection.

Kildare
County Council

Further copies available at €12, postage free, from the
above address, cheques etc. payable to DOGHOUSE also
PAYPAL - www.paypal.com to
doghousepaypal@eircom.net

Doghouse is a non-profit taking company, aiming to
publish the best of literary works by Irish or Irish
resident writers. Donations are welcome and will be
acknowledged on this page.

For our 2012 publications, many thanks to:

KERRY
EDUCATION
SERVICE
Seirbhís Oideachais Chiarraí

Kerry Education Service

Printed by Tralee Printing Works, Monavalley Industrial Estate, Tralee, Co. Kerry for Shane and Oisín

Acknowledgements are due to the editors of the following where some of these poems, or versions of them, have been published or broadcast:

An Gael (USA); The Book of Maynooth; Bringing it all Back Home (Boho Press, UK); Boyne Berries; Comhar; Cyphers; Red Hot Fiesta (Ragged Raven Press, UK); Revival; Scintilla; The SHOp; The Stony Thursday Book; Sunday Miscellany (RTÉ); Sunday Independent; The Waterford Review.

The Miracle of the Rain won the Scintilla Welsh Short Poem Poetry Competition.

Also by James Lawless:

Novels:
Peeling Oranges (2007, Killynon House, Mullingar)
For Love of Anna (2009, New Generation, UK).
The Avenue (2010, Wordsonthestreet, Galway).
Finding Penelope (2012, Indigo Dreams,UK).

Criticism:
Clearing the Tangled Wood: Poetry as a Way of Seeing the World (2009, Academica Press, USA).

Contents

Part One: Rus

Part Two: In Urbe

Part One

Rus

City Boy

How can I say
I will stay or I will go?
You left me standing
in my bare feet
on the cold stone floor.

Always querulous, I hear you say;
the birds are raucous at early light.

I do not feel the cold
on the stone floor
but a wedge pressed inside me
with fingers as light as air.

Carrying Forward

The hairs of my fingers
are caught by the sun
like some spidery creatures
and I behold the shape,
the same jutting bones,
the same freckles
which I tried to deny
and the deep caves of knuckles,
and the thin river meandering
from the wrist is his arm
and the broad mountain
is his torso
peaked by a grey-capped head
acting as an awning
for a spectacled face
and two craggy promontories
at either end
are tunnels blocked
from the hurt of years
and I recoil,
as they must have done
who beheld Lazarus,
and I cry *Father*!

Discord

Morning sun veiled
in the haze
over the dreamy sea,
waves caressing the shore;

a shout
pierces the haze,
the waves recede;

a hand picks up a stone
and hurls it at the sea
and the sea is divided
into thirty silver pieces.

Repast

The bird drills
the earth;
the orange beak
makes the worm squirm
soundlessly;

the wild cat waits
in the blooded fuchsia.

Early Light

An intruder tiptoeing,
afraid to breathe,
afraid to disturb
something deep and silent,
the only sound
the soft spray of the rain
on waterproof leaves,
no city words or whispers,
a place where birds
circle about brazenly
knowing that man is trapped
by his own fear.

Monagamas
i nGuagán Barra

Bhí pósadh sa séipéal ar an oileán;
thug an cloch foscadh don chúpla
ó cháitheadh an locha;
rinne siad a miongháire do na ceamaraí
ach ní raibh aon bhláth ar an ródaidéandran.

Dhruid na healaí i ngar dúinn
nuair a bhuaileamar ár lámha,
shíleamar an rud céanna
a athdhéanamh níos déanaí
ach thuig siad nach raibh ann
ach fuaim gan cur leis,
shín siad a muiníl agus chas siad tóin orainn
agus dhoirt siad a gcinn faoin uisce
saor ó chrá na bhfuaimeanna gan bhrí.

Is mar sin a ghreamaíonn siad le chéile,
sásta leis an leathéan céanna
ag triall i dtreo na síoraíochta,
mar tá an t-uisce acu chun a smaointe
a choimeád glan
agus cosa do-fheicthe ag tiomáint a gcroíthe.

Monogamy
at Gougane Barra

There was a wedding
at the oratory of Saint Finbar,
church stone shielded the couple
from the lake's spray
as they smiled their eternity into camera lenses,
there were no blooms on the rhododendron.

At the lake's edge the swans did not draw near
when we clapped,
they stretched their necks
and turned on their timeless journey
with water to keep their heads clear
and unseen feet propelling constantly
to drive their hearts.

Exchange

The rain drops
from the laurel leaf
to activate the sliding snail
who makes his own of the space
vacated by the rain;
his antennae
summon others
to make a feast of the leaf
and the rain finds shelter
in an abandoned shell.

Changing Forms

I wandered different roads
until I came to a garden
and there a butterfly hovered
around an apple tree;
it pirouetted and tantalised,
wings fluttering like eyelashes
on a regal mistress;
it was bold,
striking against my face
in its charade,
and then I saw something
as it ate into the fallen apple:
it was the common repast,
the human-like nibbling
that connected me,
and I thought of dead ancestors
and saw the brown of the earth.

Choices

And you prefer the mountain track
to the city street,
yet sometimes the mountain track
is too crowded for me
with its trees and flowers and birds
who peck inquisitively at me.

You see religion in every nook:
the old Mass Rock camouflaged by moss,
the Cross colonising the mountain top.

I see surfaces being scratched.
I hear lips mumbling pieties.
I behold fists talking seriously.

Room
to the memory of Emily Dickinson

How great it is
to have a place
to throw behind my back
all waste – all offal
of my human race;

it leaves the table clear
for circumference to appear

to see the atom
in the
in-between space.

Weeping as the Only Sure Course of Action

Dogs bark, drowning out
the weeping of ferns
in mountain gushes;
my toes kick off the avalanche of water
as I move upwards towards the source,
and a brightness shines
through the gloom of winter
for an instant,
and then the rain once more.

Subtraction

Ivy dying on a pier,
stone crumbling;

the skeleton of a boat
sinking into sand;

I carry the sum
all through the years:

shadows
subtracting from sunlit walls,

a child digging a hole,
taking away something
deeper than himself.

The Down

Inside:
it bursts through
the epidermis,
erupts in spots,
anchors the chest,
paralyses the tongue;
its scalpel is a loud laugh
rending me in two.

Outside:
the runny tears of trees
balm ruffled grasses.

The Bachelor Who Drank Poitín

You sang your sad song
into the night
with no applause
from the mountain;
friends came after years
to your house on the height;
they beat back the briars
and called out your name:
Jeremiah!
But your voice could not be heard.

They pushed in the door,
inhaled the putrefied air;
they called again
and a bird flew out,
alighted on a holly bush
and your corpse was found
beside four empty bottles.

Farmyard

A little sea of mud and puddle,
wellington squelch
and dogs' dirty paws
paint ogham letters
on city coats;

and smells
that overpower perfumes
of city people rarefied
by their own milieu.

Easter

A room darkened by rain and small windows,
photographs on a wall of the dead and the living,
a fly upturned on a sill,
mist obliterating the view of mountains,
leaves trembling in their new-born misery,
dogs unfettered, their fangs exposed,
heavy clouds and sheep slowrolling.
It is Easter, alone in a room,
people at church, he remembers the eve:
the clock put forward an hour, willing one to life,
but now the rain is falling,
pulling him back, clawing at him,
and the dead:
their must becomes tangible in the room.
You should laugh more, someone said.
When you laugh the past and the future disappear.
But that leaves the now,
what he sees through the window:
dogs attacking a pregnant ewe.

Sowing

Your words are wild flowers
in abandon,
dripping with sweetness
and summer rain.

You don't count the petals
or wait for the frost
to sharpen the taste
of your fruit.

Your words are
the seeds of thistles
flying in the wind
with not a care
for where they take root
or what manicured lawn
they destroy.

Old Trains

I'm walking by reeds to the gentle
accompaniment of birdsong and duckflapping
on the still water of the Royal Canal
when I hear the train
and childhood catches in my throat,
sensing a visitor
to stir the ennui of an innocent age:
my aunt, her bag laden with
Crunchies, comics and stories
to intoxicate myth-starved minds;
the steam belching,
the momentary obliteration,
doors opening,
chrome handles snapping shut
and, as the steam clears, the apparition
of my aunt waving.

The new train stops at the station,
its sound muted;
no banging of doors,
just a sliding swish;
the waiting, but no one gets off;
the train pulls away
like a fooled animal;
no steam
along the sleepers,
no choo-chooing,
no rolling stock,
just a flutter of breeze,
a heart-rending absence;
the past shimmering along the reeds.

Spinster

As I watch the river
flow around lichen-covered rocks,
I think of you, Nell,
and I realise why you used
to hold my childhand so often:
pressing a hand
held the flow of loneliness back;
in your five stone frame
the weight was in the heart.

The Pincers

The giant pincers,
a heavy instrument
of sheer steel,
shining, surgical
and yet too large
for mortal use,
a tool from Brobdingnag,
incongruous between the pudgy
fingers and dirty nails
of the roughhewn farmer.
Perhaps its purpose
was to prune the giant trees
or the wild bushes that lurk about.
It's for the bulls, he said,
handing it to me.
I felt the weight of lives
weighing me down,
in the pure light
the pincers was pristine,
flashing apocalyptic.
I opened its fangs
and saw the black hairs.

Fading Light

A crow squawks
on the dead tree of summer;
light fades

and you declare
(as your fingers move frantically)
that the seasons mean nothing,
or past time,
or solitary place;
all is headlong pursuit
of the immediate

and you say:
poetry is like knitting
a few purls.

Plucking

I always pluck the wrong things:
piss-in-the-beds,
itchy-backs,
rhubarb leaves,
sarcococca berries,
discordant strings,
stale air;
the list is endless.

You pluck wisely:
sweet apple,
ripe strawberry,
rhubarb stalks,
chords of harmony,
red rose buds;

no thorns ever pierced you
until you plucked me.

At Last the Rain has Stopped

I open the gate
which was locked for winter;
now I can go in and out
of my spring days.
The voices of children
fill the hollow
of winter's cavern
and the yawning grey light
shimmers in the stretching day;
the trees are bruised,
their foundations shaken,
but their new leaves swell with longing
and the sarcococca's scent
hints of a heaven somewhere...

Part Two

In Urbe

Ascending a Liberties' Stairway in 1952

Slate-grey steps with white ribbed bone
to steady the foot with the marks
of the washerwoman's knees
and a black iron snake to hold on to
as it coiled its way upwards,
polished smooth from the caress of hands;
and the concrete landing
where we stopped to catch our breath
and a glimpse of the stars
through a rectangular opening in an ash-grey wall
which to its side housed a handled steel door,
a chute to the Great Bin
at the bottom of the stairs,
locked in a room of its very own
where it could overflow to its heart's content
and still take more,
the extractor of all the Liberties' ills;
and the automatic light
suddenly quenched itself on the landing
– we were overstaying our time
watching the stars twinkle –
and my baby sister cried from the darkness
as we continued our ascent.
I helped my mother tilt and lift;
I could hear her heavy breathing,
each slow tortuous step its own individual,
our very own little Calvary.
The baby cried again:
Hush now, we're nearly there, alanna,* said Mam,
but we were only halfway up with the pram.

* *Alanna: vocative of Irish leanbh (child)*

Suburbia's New Day

The drone of an engine on the hill
and morning percussion on my front door,
old Mister McGinley, unshaven and dazed,
knocking to ask the name of the day.

The chestnut trees had their day;
their candles are out, a refuge gone,
just stumps now like teeth in a gaping void;
they said they were too old,
they scratched the bus,
they thwarted the growth of houses and things.

Sitting on the pavement a girl sings,
while two boys hit ball with her cripple props;
and young Freddie in his garden
caresses a machine,
polishes the shining metal,
does not hear the snarlup
or see the dead squirrel on the road.

Miss Little and Miss Browne carry their load
in plastic bags, as they shuffle along the path;
they hold each other like walking sticks,
receding from the palpable into their own dark.

I register faces in the park:
you know me, my eyes say to a young fellow,
we belong to the same classification,
but the fellow sways 'legless' on the grass,
exploring in latitudes and longitudes,
his shoulder grazes me as I pass.

And I see *them* behind glass:
they have a desk and swivel chair;
their breaths are megabytes;
their trees are figures on the VDU;
their hearts are bouncing playballs;
and they squint myopically,
the seers of the new day.

Loss
to the memory of Kit

Because you had given,
because pieces were chipped off you,
you became light
and floated above the tainted earth,
became one with the air.

The narrow boreen to the sea
without your hand in mine,
without your eyes to glimpse
the world's openings,
is blocked with brambles.

In the playground
the childhood swing
is just a chain creaking.

In the storygarden
the dreamland tree
stands lone and leafless,
shaken no more.

I am left
flapping wings
but clinging to the earth.

Sacrifice

to the memory of Jimmy

He bought Odhams Encyclopaedias on HP,
leatherbound, to be venerated by us.
Weekly payments substituted for the Friday fruit.
We consumed the pages, drank the ink.
The debt was cleared on his deathday.

He lies in the soil as I watch the covers peeling,
and in the pages I see the yellowing of his skin
beside the new Britannica.

The Mirarcle of the Rain

I undertake the *peregrinación*
out of secular curiosity.
My companion, Teresa,
on the other hand is saintly.
I met her on the road to Santiago.
She is frail and her hair is a shiny silver.
She walks discalced,
suffering calluses and cuts smilingly.
Her face is mystical, belonging to a sublime world.

I walk beside her in my sturdy walking boots
on the road to Santiago.
She carries the pilgrim's staff
and wears the scallop shell.
Of course it's only a legend, I say,
this thing about Saint James
being carried on a shell.
It's a matter of faith, she says.
You must believe things to be true
or the world is just a place of pain.
It was when the hermit Pelayo saw the great light...
And her own face lights up.
We must get there before July twenty-fifth.
El día del santo.
El día de tu santo, Jaime.
Names are fortuitous things, I say
And this year, nineteen-ninety-nine,
she says ignoring me, *is the año santo.*
Todo santo, I say mocking her.
The pilgrimage grows tiresome and difficult.
But Teresa, she carries the smile
all through the long journey.
My feet are killing me, I say,
and I am sunburnt.
That is the problem with Spain, too much sun.

You must not complain, she says
and her feet are bleeding.
The peregrinación is like life.
We must keep going.
We will be judged on how well we travelled.

We arrive at the city of Santiago
on July twenty-fifth.
We have made it, she shouts with joy,
prostrating herself on the cobbled square
in front of the cathedral,
delighting in the drizzle that has begun to fall.
A miracle, she says, trying to grasp the drops.
The miracle of the rain.
And I see the strange sight
 – people in Spain walking around
under a black sky of umbrellas.

We enter the cathedral dwarfed
like ants under its enormity.
A ceremony is taking place.
Several turifers
raise the giant *botafumeiro** with ropes.
People clap
and cameras flash from the darkness.
That's not religion, I say,
it's just a spectacle,
and why do they need it so large?
To fumigate all the unclean, she says.
Does the size of church paraphernalia
enhance religious depth?
Be quiet, James, she whispers,
and wait and pray for the miracle.
What miracle? I say.
The rain has stopped,
someone whispers from the back.

* *botafumeiro* : censer or thurible

She looks at me, no longer cheerful,
her face contorted, showing pain now
that was hidden all along,
and copious tears flow out of her eyes
as if she had gathered up
all the rain of Santiago.
She presses her pilgrim's staff
and I see the skeleton of her hand.
Pray to Santiago, she says,
that he may cure me.
And I move closer to her in the pew
and we both kneel down.

The Vanwoman Called

The ticker was skipping beats
when the vanwoman called,
swept past me with her blue toolbox,
a grunt of greeting as she headed straight
for the jugular of the mantelpiece clock;
unscrewing its face, she tore off
the diseased scions, paused at the numbers
(translating from the Roman?)
– impotent now with their indicators gone.

An alarm sounded in a neighbour's house.
The vanwoman sighed. *Is the day ever done*?
She snapped shut the face of the clock
and packed her tools into her blue toolbox,
a token smile going out the door.
You should be all right now.

An Leath Eile
do Mhairéad

Éistim leat ag comhaireamh
sa tsean-teanga,
spéaclaí ort anois,
le gile séimh tráthnóna
ag lonrú lasair-ghorm do shúile;
tá tú ag cothromú na gcuntas:
an taobh praiticiúil den animus,
chun an díon a choimeád daingean;
is tusa an tine sa tinteán;
is mise an t-uisce ag dul timpeall;
animus anima:
an cothrom faighte.

The Other Half
for Margaret

I hear you adding
in the old language,
wearing spectacles now,
the soft light
capturing in their frames
the azure of your eyes.
You are doing the accounts
to keep the roof firm,
the path clear;
you are the fire in the hearth;
I am water running through;
animus, anima:
the balance achieved.

Parisian Vignettes

The city lies muted under its evening quilt
from the steps of *Sacré Coeur;*
wisps of languages catch in the air;
the day darkens; a wind chills,
in a distant café: a half-heard love song.

A woman in a fur coat walks
a manicured poodle, *à la Degas;*
an old man squints, crouched on the arm
of his whitehaired wife,
ageing lines on his face,
charting the route of his life.

The young on skateboards parry the wind,
surfing the city's waves.
The city is movement:
the hands on the clock tower,
the feet on the pavement;
time and people pass
making space for the quotidian renewal

except in *Montmartre*
where the anatomical pictures
in their glass frames are the same every day.
The hands on the clock tower shift
as *Pigalle* litter keeps time with my feet,
while a drugged girl,
wavering in the middle of the street,
remonstrates with captive motorists.

In *Rue du Père Corentin* a woman stands all day
with a grey scarf over her head
outside a minimarket,
holding magazines and daffodils.
People without a glance step around her,
a pillar, inanimate, but in the late evening

as a misty dusk oozes into the street,
she takes out a tissue and blows her nose.

The cars are silent from the Eiffel Tower:
diminutive computer games
zigzagging in and out of lanes,
an illusion like the glass rainbows at the *Louvre*
or the middle-aged woman in the feathered hat
(a portrait by *Delacroix*?)
protesting at the unisex loo
on the grounds of inconvenience.

Near *Porte d'Orléans* is a hotel
where pigeons are barred by nets;
an immaculately groomed dog
sits statuesquely in the vestibule,
the route on the pavement
marked by his shit.

Metro: the logical labyrinth:
a one star dwelling not en suite;
whiffing the ammonia,
banishing the sweet melancholy, I surface.
My breath blows visibly through the cold air
and I follow it as a lodestar to the felt life.

Bóthar na dTaibhsí

Taistilím bóthar na dtaibhsí.
Dá dtógfá an mótarbhealach,
shroichfeá an baile níos luaithe.
Taistilím bóthar na dtaibhsí.
Dá gcasfá anseo...
An rud a deir tú, tá sé loighciúil;
is fear cliste tú;
ceapann tú nach bhfásann fréamhacha
ach faoin chré tuatha,
ach tarraingíonn bóthar na dtaibhsí mé
mar sreang an imleacáin.
Tá an tslí eile níos giorra. Tá tú ag cur ama amú.
Ach dáiríre tá mé sa bhaile cheana féin,
ar bhóthar na dtaibhsí:
an teach bán sin ar chlé,
tá taibhse mo sheanmháthar istigh ann,
agus an foirgneamh taobh thiar dúinn,
a bhí ina shéipéal tráth,
pósadh mo thuismitheoirí ansin,
agus bhí siad ina gcónaí sa teach os ár gcomhair,
an áit inar gabhadh mise
ar bhóthar na dtaibhsí;
tá lána ar dheis
a chuir deireadh le mo shoineantacht
agus boladh a mhaireann ann
de ghaolta neamh-bheo;
agus ag an gcrosbhóthar thall
chaoch an *Winking Willie* a shúil
i bhfuinneog sheomra codlata m'uncail
agus é ag casadh tóna noichte
ar chomharsana caidéiseacha.
Tá brón orm as tú a mhoilliú, a chara faoi dheifir,
ach cad tá le sonrú ar an mótarbhealach nua?
níl ann ach uaigh tarmac ag síneadh i gcéin.

Ghost Road

I travel the road of ghosts.
If you took the motorway you'd be home faster.
I travel the road of ghosts.
It's such a roundabout way.
What you say is logical;
you are an intelligent man
but still I travel the road of ghosts:
it's the pull of the umbilical cord.
But really the other way is shorter;
if you turned off here and turned right there
you'd be home in no time.
But I have plenty of time,
besides I'm already home on the road of ghosts:
that white house on the left we just passed
contains the ghost of my grandmother,
and that building back further was once a church,
the church of Saint Bernadette
where my parents were wed,
and in the house across they lived,
perhaps where I was conceived
on the road of ghosts.
The cross is where the *Winking Willie* used to wink
into the bedroom of my uncle's house
(he stuck his bare bum out that window once
at some inquisitive neighbours,
but the *Winking Willie* caught him in the act
on the road of ghosts).
There's a turn up above where my childhood ended
just off the road of ghosts.
Like sticks to like:
I smell their presence converging
on the road of ghosts.
You ask me to take the motorway,
but the motorway has buried
all its ghosts under a tarmac grave.

Cuairt Ar Gharraí Na Lus, Baile Átha Cliath

Íslíodh na hothair ón mbus
ina gcathaoireacha rothaí
ar cuairt ar Gharraí na Lus;

d'fhéach mé ar othar amháin,
ógánach le cloigeann claonta
agus béal cam;

lig an t-ógánach béic as
laistigh den teach gloine,
ag feiceáil plandaí faoi ghlas;

rug an bhanaltra greim air
agus stiúir sí amach é
le guth ard géar;

bhí an t-ógánach trí chéile
ag caitheamh a lámha
mar leanbán ar easpa céille

ag lorg ceangail
i dteanga
intuigthe do na haingil.

A Visit to the Botanic Gardens, Dublin

The automatic lift of the minibus
lowered the handicapped down in wheelchairs
on their visit to the Botanic Gardens.

One young man,
his head sideways,
his mouth lopsided,

inside the glasshouse
he shouted
on seeing the plants
in cages.

The nurse grabbed hold of him
and wheeled him out,
scolding with a sharp, high pitch.

The young man was upset,
shaking his arms
like someone without sense.

He was looking for a connection,
but talking in a language
only known to the angels.

Apex

The apex,
everything from here,
the bird perched
under the canopy of sky
monitoring with his eagle eye
the snail's pace,
the tedium of human existence.

The apex,
everything from here,
the sigh that passes up
carried by the air
to weigh down the cloud
with extra misery.

The apex,
vacant,
waiting for
something to alight
to give it meaning,
something to
connect it
to the sky
or the earth.

Calm

(in the Botanic Gardens, Dublin)

After all the winds
there is a moment
when the world rests,
the heart is calm,
there is not a ruffle
from the grass,
the water in the pond
is still as ink,
the lily leaves sleep,
the birds are muted
by a hazy sun,
the flies are the only
active ones.

Ground
a translation from the Spanish of Pedro Salinas

Ground. Nothing more.
Ground. Nothing less.
Make do with it.
Because your feet are nailed to it
and your torso to them
and on the torso a firm head
and there to the lee of one's brow
the pure thought and in the pure thought
the morrow, the key
– the morrow – of the eternal.
Ground. Neither more nor less.
Make do with it.

Christmas Eve

The birds make fake bird songs
that I heard in the Christmas shops,
the fake moon is spotted before dark,
the navy-blue sky is waiting
for its absence to be filled,
houses stand like sentries,
men in windows sharpen knives,
dogs bark at the fading light,
black specks of carbon birds
circle my head
because I am one
who will not look up,
the small boy counts down,
radio and TV hop with expectation,
the weather changes,
the bookmaker gives good odds on snow,
all is meant to change,
the barometer moves up and down
the human heart,
cloying melodies bring tears
to those who depart;
it is a time of arrival
where the moss grows green
and the harvest that was gathered
can now be shared between
the angels carrying candles
and the drunk who sways in the wind.

The Cut and Thrust of Life

Before the hernia operation
the surgeon adjusted the sac.
It should hang so so, should it not?
All the desires,
all the times of individualising
one's own genitals
reduced to this:
a mathematical proposition.

On Meeting a Novice in Sacerdotal Cloth in Maynooth

The virginal look of the blond boy:
such perfect skin,
such clear eyes,
such white teeth
to blend with the radiant collar,
such innocence
to hurl upon a world
gone stale,
as if time long gone
had decided to return,
and the pristine quality of the cloth,
the shining black
perched on such an old dogma.

The Tramp in the Lady

Crisp cursive curlicues
camouflage your dirty ink;

your pinny
covers soiled garments;

the rims of your spectacles
stab at the stars;

your hair in a bun
is a birdless nest;

such neatness
hearts froze,
you are the prim
without the rose.

The Hero Myth

A crow in a flock
squawks at the lone eagle
soaring high,
a Hollywood myth
of Greece and Rome
and ancient Ireland
of Cúchulainn and Fionn
and Aeneas and Hercules
and John Wayne and Clint Eastwood,
all the bravery of a delirium,
the mythological conundrum
of the lone ranger
in a world
of palm-chin whisperers
and brown-tongued vipers.

Automaton

No, nothing,
not even a kiss
to plant my feet on,
ground, nothing else
to walk away on,
arms to stretch out for,
dangling dummies.

Find the key
to wind me up
to set me in
the right direction
towards the
clockwork girl.

Dying by the Mediterranean

I could die easily reclining on a chair
near the Mediterranean
in the evening,
after an inexpensive *Rioja* or *San Miguel*
where the balmy waves soothe.

And yet my eyes
push back the downfalling blinds
and a salty trickle of sweat
taunts at my lips.

But still... and still
I have the count of the waves
and the Mediterranean,
my darkening companion,
sheds its white sperm
and spends itself on the shore.

Why is the Future Sinister?

The tramp stands
with snowflaked eyebrows
outside the frosted window,
holding a knife and a cut slice of bread
while George dances the boogaloo
and Beverley swings her hips.

Swishing blades rotate
as more revellers land on the helipad,
heads stooped in their frippery,
marking their territory
with *Yves Saint Laurent*.

The tramp takes fright
from his breath's spyhole,
just a boy with a worldworn face,
bounding over the lawn
stabbing the air with his knife.

Bored Meeting

I am alive among the bodies at meetings:
trapdoor mouths open and snap shut,
gnarled words evaporate into hot air,
but the pulse is not here;
it is keeping time to other music
somewhere in the forest floor.

James Lawless was born in Dublin and divides his time between County Kildare and West Cork. He is the author of the novels *Peeling Oranges* (Killynon House, 2007), *For Love of Anna* (New Generation, 2009) and *The Avenue* (Wordsonthestreet, 2010), and a study of modern poetry, *Clearing the Tangled Wood: Poetry as a Way of Seeing the World* (Academica Press, USA, 2009).

Awards include the Scintilla Welsh Open Poetry Competition, the Cecil Day Lewis Award, the Sunday Tribune/Hennessy and Willesden Herald award nominations, the WOW Award and a Biscuit International prize for short stories. His latest novel, *Finding Penelope*, is published in 2012 in the UK by Indigo Dreams.

www.jameslawless.net

Also available from DOGHOUSE:

Heart of Kerry – an anthology of writing
from performers at Poet's Corner, Harty's Bar, Tralee
1992-2003
Song of the Midnight Fox – Eileen Sheehan
Loose Head & Other Stories – Tommy Frank
O'Connor
Both Sides Now - Peter Keane
Shadows Bloom / Scáthanna Faoi Bhláth – haiku by
John W. Sexton, translations, Gabriel Rosenstock
FINGERPRINTS (On Canvas) – Karen O'Connor
Vortex – John W. Sexton
Apples in Winter – Liam Aungier
The Waiting Room – Margaret Galvin
I Met a Man... Gabriel Rosenstock
The DOGHOUSE book of Ballad Poems
The Moon's Daughter – Marion Moynihan
Whales off the Coast of my Bed – Margaret O'Shea
PULSE – Writings on Sliabh Luachra – Tommy Frank
O'Connor
A Bone in my Throat – Catherine Ann Cullen
Morning at Mount Ring – Anatoly Kudryavitsky
Lifetimes – Folklore from Kerry
Kairos – Barbara Smith
Planting a Mouth – Hugh O'Donnell
Down the Sunlit Hall – Eileen Sheehan
New Room Windows – Gréagóir Ó Dúill
Slipping Letters Beneath the Sea – Joseph Horgan
Canals of Memory – Áine Moynihan
Arthur O'Leary & Arthur Sullivan – Musical Journeys
from Kerry to the Heart of Victorian England - Bob
Fitzsimons
Crossroads – Folklore from Kerry
Real Imaginings – a Kerry anthology, edited by
Tommy Frank O'Connor

Touching Stones – Liam Ryan
Where the Music Comes From – Pat Galvin
No Place Like It – Hugh O'Donnell
The Moon Canoe – Jerome Kiely
An Exhalation of Starlings - Tom Conaty
Via Crucis - David Butler
Capering Moons – Anatoly Kudryavitsky
I Shouldn't be Telling You This – Mae Leonard
Notes Towards a Love Song – Aidan Hayes
Between the Lines – Karen O'Connor
Watching Clouds - Gerry Boland
Meeting Mona Lisa - Tommy Frank O'Connor
Asking for Directions – Michael Farry
The Angel's Share – Barbara Smith
Outward and Return – Gréagóir O Dúill
Slow Mysteries – Monica Corish
Bamboo Dreams - an Anthology of Haiku from
Ireland – edited by Anatoly Kudryavitsky
The Sear of Wounds – Mark Whelan

Every DOGHOUSE book costs €12, postage free,
to anywhere in the world (& other known planets).
Cheques, Postal Orders (or any legal method) payable
to DOGHOUSE, also PAYPAL (www.paypal.com) to
doghousepaypal@eircom.net

"Buy a full set of DOGHOUSE books, in time they will be
collectors' items" - Gabriel Fitzmaurice, April 12, 2005.
DOGHOUSE
P.O. Box 312
Tralee G.P.O.
Tralee
Co. Kerry
Ireland
tel + 353 6671 37547
email doghouse312@eircom.net
www.doghousebooks.ie